# Collins English



Series editors: K R Cripwell and L

A library of graded readers for stuc
language, and for reluctant native readers. ...
of difficulty. Structure, vocabulary, idiom and sentence length are all controlled according to principles laid down in detail in *A Guide to Collins English Library*. A list of the books follows. Numbers after each title indicate the level at which the book is written: 1 has a basic vocabulary of 300 words and appropriate structures, 2 : 600 words, 3 : 1000 words, 4 : 1500 words, 5 : 2000 words and 6: 2500 words.

*Inspector Holt and the Fur Van* John Tully 1
*Where is Bill Ojo?* John Tully 1
*Crocodile!* K R Cripwell 1
*Four Short Stories* Margery Morris 1
*The Story of Macbeth* from Shakespeare 1
*Fast Money* K R Cripwell 1
*It's a Trick!* Lewis Jones 1
*Taxi!* Jane Homeshaw 1
*Tin Lizzie* Jane Homeshaw 1
*Dead in the Morning* Jane Homeshaw 1
*Letters from the Dead* Jane Homeshaw 1
*The Pathfinders* Jane Homeshaw 1
*Cats in the Dark* John Tully 1
*Journey to Universe City* Leslie Dunkling 1
*Three Folk Tales* Margaret Naudi 1
*Inspector Holt and the Chinese Necklace* John Tully 1
*Inspector Holt Gets His Man* John Tully 2
*The Bridge* John Tully 2
*Muhammad Ali: King of the Ring* John Tully 2
*The Magic Garden* K R Cripwell 2
*The Wrestler* K R Cripwell 2
*The Titanic is Sinking* K R Cripwell 2
*The Canterville Ghost* Oscar Wilde 2
*The Prince and the Poor Boy* Mark Twain 2
*Two Roman Stories* from Shakespeare 2
*Oliver Twist* Charles Dickens 2
*The Story of Madame Tussaud's* Lewis Jones 2
*Three Sherlock Holmes Adventures* Sir A Conan Doyle 2
*The Story of Scotland Yard* Lewis Jones 2
*Charles and Diana* Margery Morris 2
*The Charlie Chaplin Story* Jane Homeshaw 2
*A King's Love Story* K R Cripwell 2
*Dangerous Earth* Jane Homeshaw 2
*Chariots of Fire* W J Weatherby 2
*Shark Attack!* Jan Keane 2
*The Complete Robot: Selected Stories* Isaac Asinov 2
*Five Ghost Stories* Viola Huggins 3

*Brainbox and Bull* Michael Kenyon 3
*Climb a Lonely Hill* Lilith Norman 3
*Custer's Gold* Kenneth Ulyatt 3
*The Gunshot Grand Prix* Douglas Rutherford 3
*Born Free* Joy Adamson 3
*Cinema Stunts* K R Cripwell 3
*David Copperfield* Charles Dickens 3
*Three English Kings* from Shakespeare 3
*An American Tragedy* Theodore Dreiser 3
*Six American Stories* Norman Wymer 3
*Emma and I* Sheila Hocken 3
*Maimunah* David Hill 3
*Little Women* Louisa M Alcott 3
*Marilyn Monroe* Peter Dainty 3
*Bruce Springsteen* Toni Murphy 3
*The Picture of Dorian Gray* Oscar Wilde 3
*The White South* Hammond Innes 4
*Landslide* Desmond Bagley 4
*Nothing is the Number when you Die* Joan Fleming 4
*The Lovely Lady and Other Stories* D H Lawrence 4
*King Solomon's Mines* H Rider Haggard 4
*A Christmas Carol* Charles Dickens 4
*Jane Eyre* Charlotte Bronte 4
*Pride and Prejudice* Jane Austen 4
*Dr Jekyll and Mr Hyde* R L Stevenson 4
*Huckleberry Finn* Mark Twain 4
*The African Child* Camara Laye 4
*Tiger* Kailash Sankhala 4
*Airport International* Brian Moynahan 4
*The Secret Sharer and Other Sea Stories* Joseph Conrad 4
*Death in Vienna* K E Rowlands 4
*Hostage Tower* Alistair MacLean/John Denis 4
*The Guns of Navarone* Alistair MacLean 5
*Where Eagles Dare* Alistair MacLean 5
*I Know my Love* Catherine Gaskin 5
*The Wreck of the Mary Deare* Hammond Innes 5
*The Eagle has Landed* Jack Higgins 5
*Geordie* David Walker 5
*Among the Elephants* Iain and Oria Douglas-Hamilton 5
*The Mayor of Casterbridge* Thomas Hardy 5
*Wuthering Heights* Emily Bronte 5
*Sense and Sensibility* Jane Austen 5
*Middlemarch* George Eliot 5
*Victory* Joseph Conrad 5
*Experiences of Terror* Roland John 5
*Japan: Islands in the Mist* Peter Milward 5
*House of a Thousand Lanterns* Victoria Holt 6
*The Glory Boys* Gerald Seymour 6
*Harry's Game* Gerald Seymour 6
*Inspector Ghote Breaks an Egg* H R F Keating 6
*Hard Times* Charles Dickens 6
*In the Shadow of Man* Jane Goodall 6
*Doctor Zhivago* Boris Pasternak 6
*Sons and Lovers* D H Lawrence 6
*The Dark Frontier* Eric Ambler 6
*Vanity Fair* William Thackeray 6

Collins English Library Level 3

# Born Free

## JOY ADAMSON

Abridged and simplified by Norah Woollard

Illustrations by Susan O'Carroll

Collins: London and Glasgow

Printed and published in Great Britain by
William Collins Sons and Co Ltd
Glasgow G4 0NB



First published in Collins English Library, 1979

We are grateful to Photo Library International – Leeds for permission to reproduce the photograph which appears on the cover.

6 7 8 9 10

# 1 New Babies

This story has its beginning on a journey in Kenya. A man was killed there by a man-eating lion, and the report came to my husband George.

Our home is near Isiolo, about 200km north-east of Nairobi. My husband's job is to look after the wildlife in the northern part of Kenya. He must stop unlawful killing of certain animals. He also has to hunt dangerous animals that have attacked people from the villages.

I like to travel with him when he makes a long journey. In this way I have learned a lot about the nature of this wild, unchanged land.

The report said that the man-eating lion was living in some nearby hills. Two lionesses were living with him. And so it became George's job to hunt them down. This was why we were camping far to the north of Isiolo among the Boran people, in February, some years ago.

One morning I was alone in the camp. Suddenly I heard the sound of a car. George was

returning much earlier than he planned. Soon our Landrover appeared across the dry rocky land. The Landrover stopped and I heard George shout:

"Joy, where are you? Quick, I have something for you...."

I ran out and saw the skin of a lion. But before I could ask about the hunt, George pointed to the back of the car. There were three lion cubs, only a few weeks old. Their eyes were still covered with a thin blue skin. They couldn't walk, but they tried to hide their faces from us.

I took them into my arms to comfort them while George told me the story.

"It was dark when we got near the man-eater's hiding-place. When first light broke, a lioness ran out from behind some rocks. She came straight at us. I had no wish to kill her, but I had to shoot to save myself.

"She was a big lioness and her teats were heavy with milk. When I saw that, I realised that she must have some young cubs somewhere. We listened for their cries and soon found them in a deep hole in the rocks. We carried them to the car – and here they are!"

It was two days before the cubs learned to drink milk from a bottle. We took a soft bit of rubber off the radio to make a sort of teat for the bottle.

When, at last, the cubs accepted the milk, they could not get enough of it. Every two hours I had to heat the milk and clean the home-made teat.

The nearest African market was about eighty kilometres away. We sent someone to buy a real baby's bottle and a real teat. At the same time we sent a letter to our home at Isiolo, about 240km away. We told them the news of our three 'babies', and asked for a comfortable wooden home for them on our return.

## 2 Cub Life

I loved the smallest cub best. She was the weakest, but she was the bravest of the three. I called her Elsa.

If they had stayed in the wild Elsa would be dead. A lioness usually has four cubs. One dies soon after birth and another is often too weak to live long. It is for this reason that you usually see only two cubs with a lioness.

Their mother looks after them until they are two years old. For the first year she brings their food. She eats it herself first and then she brings it up again. In this way the cubs can manage the food.

Lions often live together in a group called a 'pride'. The full-grown lions of the pride do the hunting and killing. During their second year the cubs hunt with the pride but they are unable to kill on their own. They only eat what the big lions leave. Often very little remains for them, so they are usually in a bad, thin condition at this age.

Sometimes the hunger is too much for the cubs. They try to take the meat before the adults have finished eating. The big lions will kill them for this. Sometimes the hungry cubs will leave the pride in small groups. And because they do not yet know how to kill, they often run into trouble. Nature's law is hard and lions have to learn the hard way from the beginning.

In the wild, Elsa would be the throw-out of the pride. At five months old, living with us, she was in fine condition. But she was still weaker than the other two cubs. They fought over every meal and poor Elsa did not get enough. I kept bits of meat for her and took her on to my knee for her meals. I played with her while I fed her and she loved this. During these hours a deep feeling grew between us.

We could not keep three fast-growing lions for ever. Sadly, we decided that the two big ones must go. I chose to keep Elsa and everyone in the house agreed. Perhaps they were thinking: "If there must be a lion in the house, it should be as small as possible."

We sent the two biggest cubs away to Europe. Poor Elsa searched everywhere for her sisters. She followed George and me everywhere. I think she feared we might leave her too.

We kept her in the house to make her feel safe. She slept on our bed at night. We were often woken by her rough tongue washing our faces.

Something soon happened to help Elsa forget her sadness; she met her first elephant.

One day our boy, Nuru, took her out for her morning walk. He came running back to the house alone.

"Come quickly," he said. "Elsa is playing with an elephant!"

We took our guns and followed him to the place.

A great old elephant had his head in a tree. He was enjoying his breakfast. Suddenly, Elsa ran up behind him and took a playful bite at one of his legs. The elephant turned with a loud scream of anger and surprise. Elsa jumped quickly out of his way as he ran at her. She was not a bit afraid. She began to walk behind him like a hunter.

It was a worrying moment. Elsa had no mother to explain the danger. Elephants look upon lions as the only enemies of their young – and so they sometimes try to kill them.

Luckily, after a time, both became tired of the

game. The old elephant went back to his meal and Elsa lay down, close by, and went to sleep.

Every year, at this time, several hundred elephants pass through Isiolo. The great animals seem to know all about the town. They always go to the places where the best vegetables grow. But they do not cause much other trouble among all the people and the motor traffic in the town.

Our home is only four kilometres from Isiolo and so we get many of these large visitors. We have to be careful on our walks in the country because small groups of elephants are always about. And now, with Elsa, we had to be more careful than ever.

We were having lunch one day when a long line of elephants crossed the open land in front of our house. One by one, about twenty elephants passed our dining-room window. At the end of the line came Elsa. She held her head low and her tail straight out.

The big elephant in front of her turned his great head and gave a loud high scream. This war-cry did not worry Elsa and she followed the elephants into the trees.

It was too dangerous to go out and try to bring Elsa home. We could see the shapes of elephants in all directions. There were no screams, nor any sounds of breaking branches. But I was very worried until our young cub returned safely to us.

Life became even more exciting when a rhino

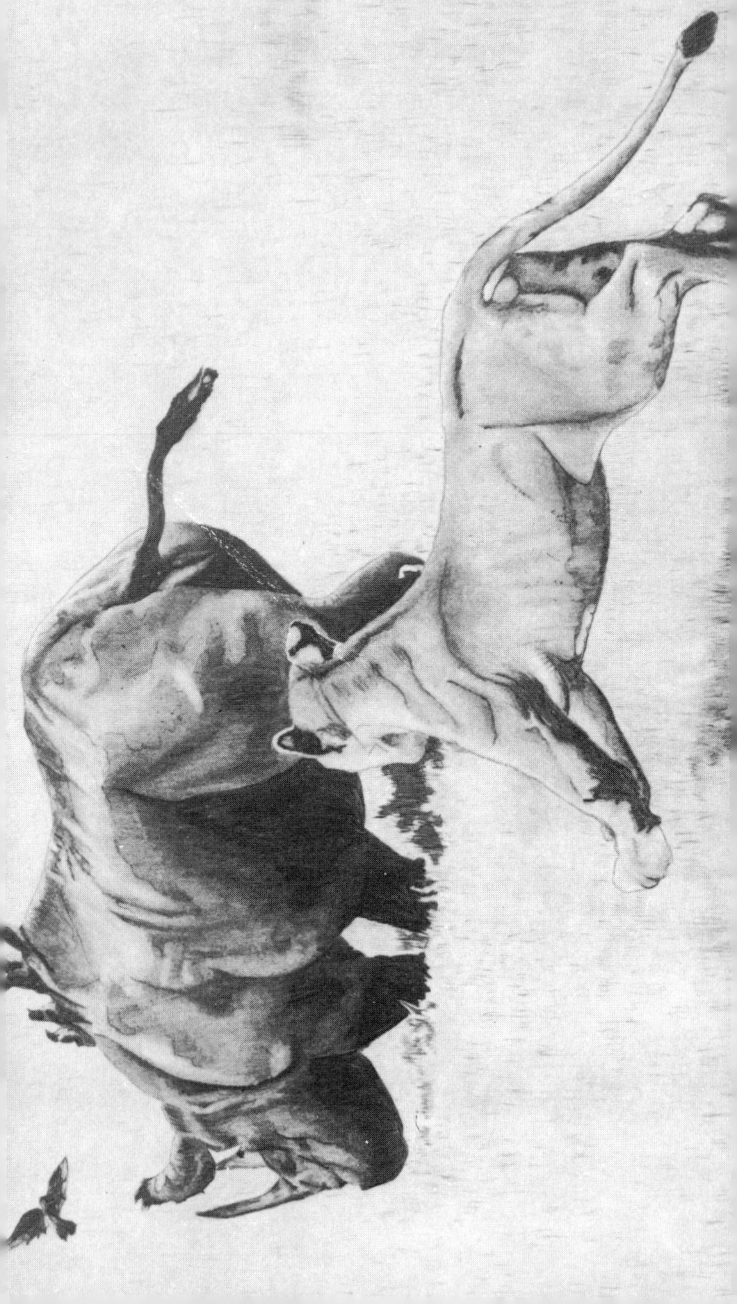

came to live near our house. I was walking with Elsa and Nuru one evening. We were late and it was getting dark. Suddenly, Nuru caught my arm and stopped me. I was walking straight into a rhino which was standing behind a tree looking at us. I jumped back and ran.

Rhinos are dangerous animals. They will attack anything, even lorries and trains. Luckily Elsa did not see the rhino. She thought I was playing a game, thank goodness! So she followed me out of danger.

But the next day Elsa had her fun. She surprised the rhino behind the house. He ran off and she ran after him for four or five kilometres across the valley. Like a true friend, Nuru ran behind her. After this, the rhino left to find a quieter living place.

## 3 Elsa Meets other Lions

Elsa's days were happy ones. The mornings were cool; we often sat together and watched the impala antelopes. As the birds awoke we listened to their morning song. As soon as it got light Nuru took Elsa out for a short walk. The cub was always full of life. She ran after everything she could find. She even chased her own tail.

Then, when the sun got warm, she and Nuru sat under a leafy tree. Elsa slept while Nuru read his Koran and drank tea.

Nuru always carried a gun to keep off wild animals. But we told him: "Call out before you shoot", and he was very good about this.

About tea-time, the two of them returned home. Elsa then stayed with George and me for the rest of the day. First she had some milk. Then we went walking into the hills. She climbed trees and chased any animal we met. She wanted to play games all the time with us. We were now her 'pride'.

As darkness fell we returned home. Elsa's evening meal was waiting for her. She had large pieces of uncooked meat. I held the bones for her and she ate them from my fingers.

Fed and happy, Elsa often went to sleep with my thumb in her mouth. It was only on moonlight nights that she became restless. Then she walked beside the wall; backwards and forwards, listening carefully. She lifted her nose to smell the mysteries of the night outside.

But as Elsa grew, her restlessness also grew. Sometimes she refused to return home with us from her evening walks. She wanted to spend the night out in the country. We had to drive to her in the Landrover and bring her back. In fact, she soon decided that it was a waste of time to walk home. So she jumped on to the soft roof of the car and rode home in comfort. This was all very nice for the lioness but not very good for the car! George soon had to fit a stronger roof.

Elsa was now a two-year old lioness and her voice changed to a deep growl. She began to show signs that she was ready for sex and wanted to mate with a lion. She did not let us choose the way for our walks; she wanted to cross the valley. One afternoon she led us in her direction and we soon found the fresh marks of a wild lion. At dark she refused to return.

"Let's go and get the Landrover," said George. We walked back to the house.

"I'll stay here," I said. "Elsa might come back a different way."

But Elsa did not come home on her own and George came back without her.

"She's been gone for two hours now," I told him. "Will you try again?"

George left again and soon after I heard a shot. Until he came back I was very worried. I was even more worried when he told me the result of his search.

"I drove slowly, calling for Elsa for about half an hour," said George. "But she didn't come. Then I stopped the car in an open space, wondering where to look next. Suddenly, some two hundred metres behind the car there was a loud noise of lions fighting. Then, the next moment, a lioness raced by, followed by another. As they shot past I managed to put a bullet under the second animal. I think it was Elsa that she was running after.

"I jumped into the car and drove after them. But I was soon forced to stop. A lion and two lionesses stood in my way. They were making a lot of noise, growling loudly. I couldn't do anything!

"Come on. I'll show you where it happened."

We drove back to the place and we called and called for Elsa. No friendly growl came in answer. Then, after a while, the loud cries of lions started a few hundred metres away. We drove towards them until we could see three sets of eyes shining.

There was nothing more to do. So, with heavy hearts, we turned for home. Would Elsa be killed by the angry lioness? In her present condition she might easily mate with the lion. His own lioness might not like that.

Then two kilometres along our way we saw Elsa smelling at a tree. She did not even look at us. We called her to the car but she remained still. She kept looking wishfully in the direction of the lions.

Presently they started calling again and came near. Thirty metres behind us was a dry river bed and here the pride stopped, growling loudly. It was now after midnight. Elsa sat in the moonlight

between the lions and us. Both parties called her to their side. Who was going to win?

Suddenly Elsa moved towards the lions and I cried out:

"Elsa! No! Don't go there. You'll get killed!"

She sat down again looking at us and looking back at her own kind. She did not know what to do. An hour passed and nothing changed. Then George sent two shots over the lions. This had the effect of sending them off in silence.

Elsa still couldn't decide between the two parties. We drove slowly back home hoping that she might follow us. Very coolly she walked alongside the car, looking back many times. Till, at last, she jumped on to the roof of the car and we brought her safely back. When we arrived home she was very tired and thirsty and drank without stopping.

"She's been with those lions for five hours," said George looking at the clock. "I wonder what happened? Did the pride accept her with the smell of men on her?"

"And why did she return to us instead of going with her own kind?" I said. "Was it because she was afraid of the angry lioness?"

Elsa was safe and well after her adventure. But how I wished she could answer the questions that we asked ourselves.

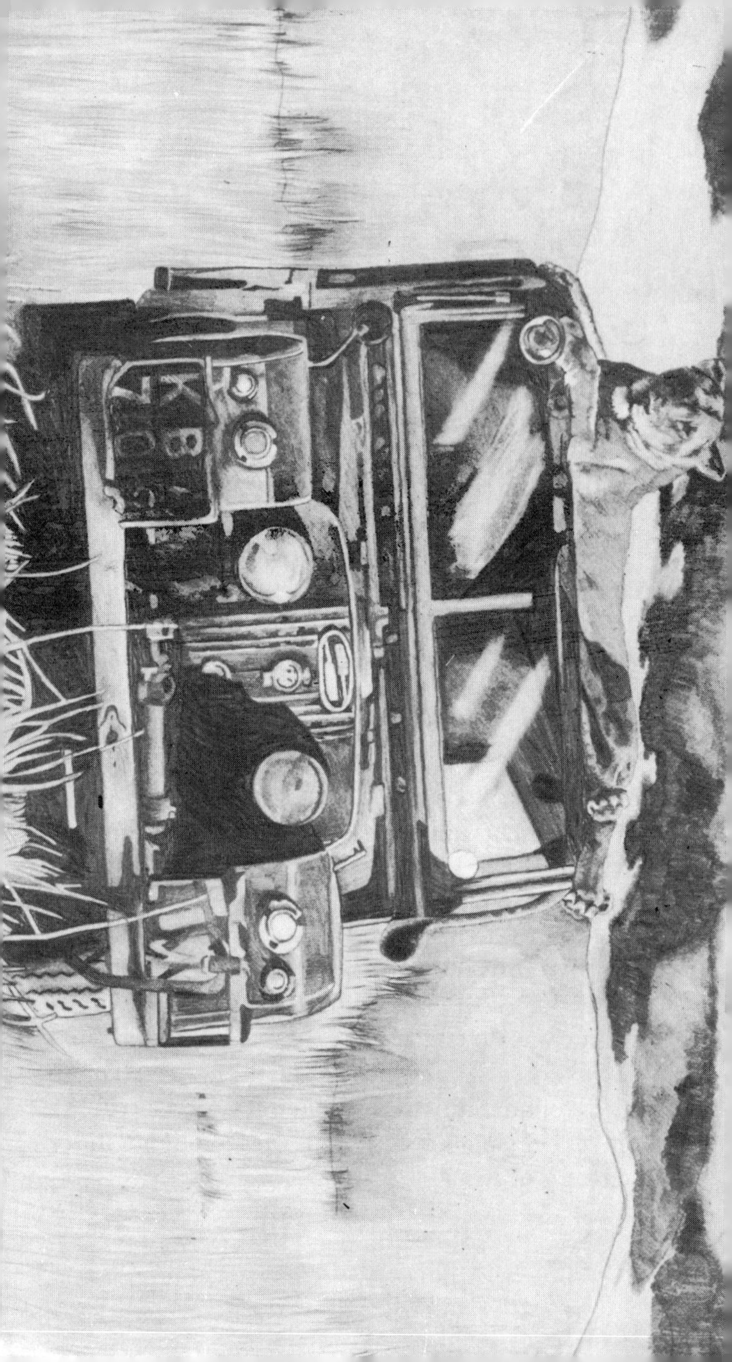

# 4 New Country

The call of the wild seemed to grow stronger and stronger. Often Elsa did not return with us at dark and we spent many evenings looking for her. In the dry weather, water was our strongest hold on her because she could only get it at the house. But soon the rains would come....

Two and a half months after her adventure with the wild lions Elsa was again in a mating condition. Her body had a strange smell. She would not let Nuru walk with her into the hills. When he tried to follow her she growled at him and went off quickly among the rocks.

After the midday heat we went out and called to her. An answer came – a strange growl. It was not Elsa's voice, it was a wild lion. Soon afterwards Elsa came down the hill to us, calling in her usual way. When she reached us she threw herself on to the ground. She was tired out but very excited. We gave her some water and she could not have enough of it.

Now we noticed several bloody marks on her back legs, and her neck. There were also teeth marks on her head. She now had a very strong smell.

When she felt better she was as friendly as usual. She came and talked to each of us. She was very pleased with herself and seemed to be saying: "Listen to what I have learned."

From this time onwards Elsa spent more and more time away. Sometimes she was away, without food or water, for two or three days. Then hunger and thirst brought her back to us. We realised that when the rains came we would lose our hold on her.

Elsa was now twenty-seven months old, almost fully grown. "We have to decide soon about her future," I said to George. "We can't leave her here when we go away on holiday."

"Well, we have always known that we can't keep her here for ever at Isiolo," he answered. "We must let her go."

"But will she be accepted by other lions?" I said. "She carries the smell of men and she hasn't learned to hunt and kill. She might be killed if she tries to join a pride."

"I know that is what usually happens to animals who have lived with men," George answered. "But Elsa has been lucky. She has lived in her own country. She has met plenty of wild animals. And now she has mated. I think she has a

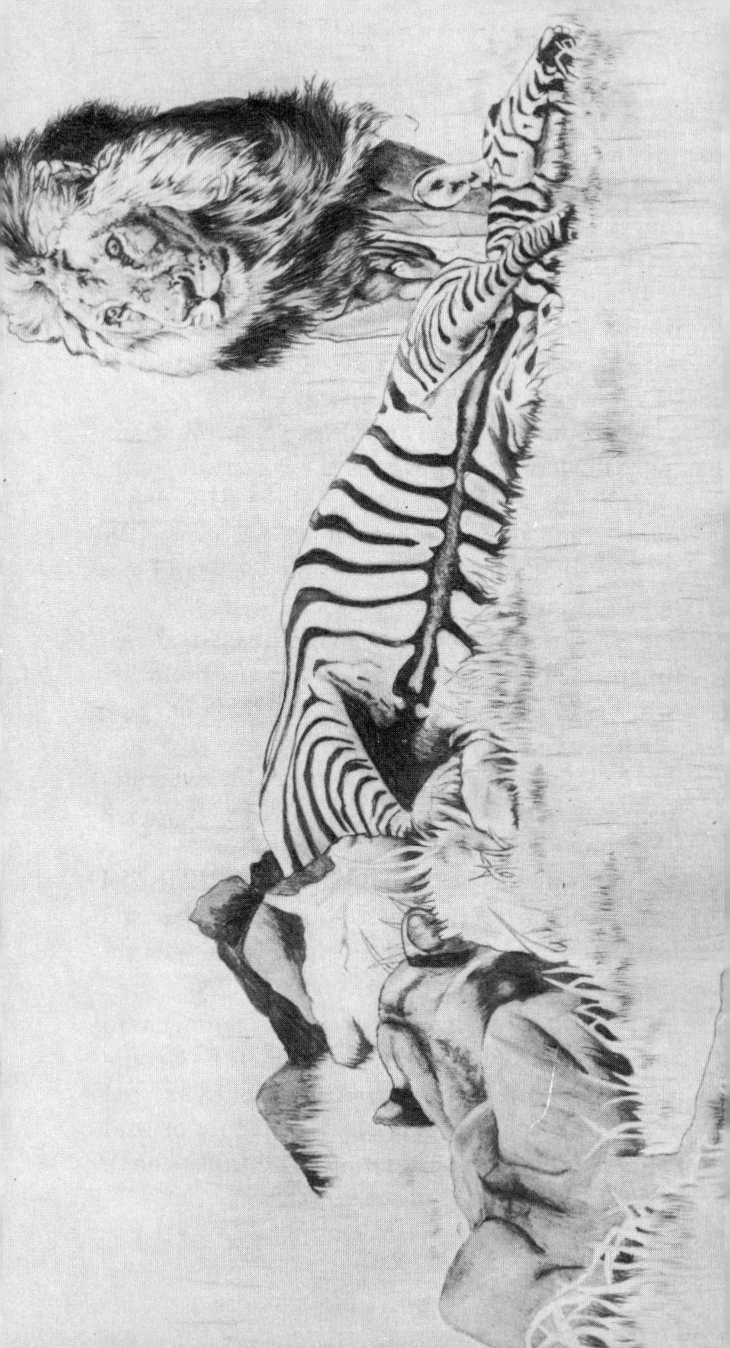

good chance."

In the end we decided to spend two or three weeks teaching Elsa to live without us. Then, if all went well, we would take a holiday.

Next we had to think, *where* to let Elsa go free. There were too many people around Isiolo. It was not fair to let her go wild there. But we knew a part of the country where few people lived but where many wild animals lived.

Our plan was this: we would spend the first week taking Elsa round the new country. She could travel on the roof of the Landrover. In this way she would get to know the land. It is much higher than her homeland in the Northern Frontier – about 1500 metres above the sea. She would also see some animals which do not live in our part of Kenya.

During the second week we planned to leave her to run free at night. We would visit her and feed her in the mornings when she was sleepy. Afterwards we would feed her less often. Then, we hoped, she would kill on her own or find a wild lion mate.

After resting from the long journey we began to put our plan into action. One morning we went out and soon found a lion on a zebra kill. He was hungrily eating the zebra meat and took no notice of us. Elsa slowly got down from the car and walked carefully towards him.

At last the lion looked up and straight at Elsa.

He seemed to say: "How dare you, woman, come near the king of animals when he is having his meal? Don't you know lion law? You may kill for me, but you must wait for me to finish. Then you may eat up what I leave."

Elsa did not like the look he gave her. She returned as fast as she could to her safe seat on the car roof. The great lion continued feeding on the zebra. We watched him for a long time hoping that Elsa might feel brave again. But she would not leave her seat.

Next morning we had better luck. We found a young lion resting in the high grass, sunning himself. He was a beautiful animal. Just the right husband for Elsa, we thought.

We drove to within thirty metres of him. He seemed a little surprised when he saw a lioness sitting on top of a car. But he looked friendly. Elsa showed her interest by making soft low growls, but she would not come off the roof. So we drove a little way off and managed to get her down to the ground. Then, suddenly, we left her and drove round to the other side of the lion. This meant she would have to pass him to reach us.

After much painful thought, Elsa was brave enough to walk towards the lion. When she was about ten steps away from him she lay down with her ears back and her tail waving. The lion got up and went towards her. I am sure it was a friendly move; but at the last moment Elsa was afraid and ran back to the car.

We drove away with her. And, strangely enough, we came right to a pride of two lions and one lioness. They were on a kill.

Elsa called to them. But they were so busy with their meal that they took no notice of her. When they were full, they left the kill and walked off. Elsa lost no time in trying some of the meat. It was her first sight of a real kill, and it was just what we wanted for her. A meal, killed by lions, and full of their fresh smell.

When Elsa finished eating we took the kill back to the friendly young lion. We hoped that he would think well of Elsa if she brought him a meal. Then we left her and the kill near to him and drove off.

After a few hours we were going to see what was happening, but we met Elsa already half-way back to our camp. We thought it was a good idea to try again and we took her back to the lion. We found him still in the same place. Elsa talked to him from her seat like an old friend. But she would not go to him.

We drove behind a rock and stopped. I was going to pull Elsa from her seat when we saw a newly killed baby zebra. It must be the lion's kill.

Elsa was hungry. She forgot her fears and jumped off the car on to the meat. We drove away as fast as we could and left her alone for her night's adventure. And early next morning we went out to visit her, hoping to find two happy animals.

Instead, we found poor Elsa waiting at the same rock, but without the lion and without the kill. She was so pleased to see us and wanted so much to stay with us! She ran her rough tongue over my fingers again and again to make sure that everything was all right between us. I was very unhappy about hurting her feelings. I wished I could explain that we had done it for her own good.

After a time she seemed happier and she felt safe enough with us to fall asleep. Sadly, we decided that we must leave her again and we went quietly away.

## 5 Life beside the River

At Isiolo we always cut up Elsa's meat before we gave it to her. We did not want her to know that her food came from living animals. But now we needed to teach her just this. So we shot a small buck for her and brought her the whole animal. We wondered if she would know how to open it.

She had no mother to teach her the right way of doing it.

We soon saw that she knew exactly what to do with the buck. She started at the inside part of the back legs where the skin is softest. Then she bit open the buck's body and ate the good bits inside. She dug a hole in the ground for the parts she did not want to eat. And then she covered up the blood as all wild lions do. She ate the rest of the meat with her back teeth. Lastly, she cleaned off the bones with her rough tongue.

When we knew that she could do this, it was time to let Elsa do her own killing. We started to leave her alone for two or three days at a time. We hoped that hunger would force her to kill. But when we came back we always found her waiting for us and hungry.

It was heart-breaking to see her so unhappy, but we knew it was for her own good. She had to learn to feed herself.

But the weeks went by and it seemed that Elsa would not learn to kill on her own. We thought that she might be unhappy in this type of country. It was very different from the country of her birth. George knew of a place that would suit her better. It was much lower land, greener and hotter too. And so we moved and made a new camp near a wide, slow-moving river.

It was clear that Elsa needed a teacher. We do not like killing animals, but Elsa had to learn from

us. George started to take her out hunting with him.

One morning they came upon a waterbuck and George shot it. But before the buck fell, Elsa jumped at its neck and held on with her teeth. In a few minutes the animal died. It was Elsa's first kill of a large animal. We now saw that she knew exactly where to bite the buck's neck. A lion does not usually break an animal's neck, but stops its breath. Elsa did not need to be taught this. We were very glad that she knew how to end the animal's life quickly and cleanly.

She opened the buck between the back legs and ate the soft insides. Carefully, she covered the blood and the unwanted parts with earth, and pulled the buck into the shade of a nearby tree. We left her there to look after her kill.

About teatime we went back to visit her and brought her water. She usually loved to walk with us, but this time she would not leave her kill. When it became dark she did not return to the camp. But about three in the morning we were awakened by a heavy fall of rain. Soon after this Elsa appeared and spent the rest of the night in camp.

Later in the morning we all went out to find her kill. Of course it was gone and the ground was marked by lions. Nearby we heard some lion growls. Was it the rain or the lions that made Elsa leave her kill during the night?

Sometimes George took Elsa out fishing with him. As he fished, Elsa sat and watched carefully for the smallest movement in the water. As soon as George caught a fish, she splashed into the river to get it. Sometimes she ran straight back to camp with the fish. There she usually dropped the fish on George's bed. She seemed to say: "This cold, strange kill is yours." She then returned to the river to wait for the next catch.

Close to the river stood a great tree, with its branches nearly touching the water. Its cool green shade kept out the burning sun. I often hid here and watched many wild animals which came to the river to drink. I thought this would be a good place for painting and writing. We made a table and a seat from some wooden boxes and fixed them under the wide branches.

Elsa pushed her nose into my paintbox and my typewriter. She did not like these things which took me from her. She washed my face, wanting to be sure of my love. Then she lay down at my feet and let me start work.

I did not know it before but there were watchers close by. When I tried to write I heard the sound of a baboon. Then the tree on the other side of the river became alive with interested watching faces. Soon the baboons became braver and began jumping from tree to tree. They screamed at Elsa and called out to each other. And all the while they danced like shadows in the tree-tops.

Until one little baboon fell with a splash into the river. At once an old baboon came to save it, and raced off with the wet unhappy animal. When this happened the screaming from all the other baboons was unbelievable.

Elsa could not take the noise any longer. She splashed into the river and swam across. The baboons were greatly amused at this and screamed with laughter. As soon as Elsa reached dry ground she jumped up at the nearest baboon. He climbed quickly to a higher branch just out of Elsa's reach. From this safe place he pulled faces and shook the branch at Elsa. As the lioness became more and more angry, more baboons began to play the same game.

The sight was so funny that I opened my cine camera and filmed it. But Elsa never did like cameras and this was just too much! When she saw me point the camera at her she splashed back through the river. Before I could fasten the camera she jumped on me. We both fell in the sand together with the camera. Everything was wet. The baboons screamed with laughter at the show. They clearly thought we weren't very clever at all.

# 6 Elsa Finds a Mate

During these happy times we could forget that we had to teach Elsa to be a killer. But each day we continued with her lessons. One day George shot a buffalo which came near our camp. We hoped that such a large animal would bring wild lions to the kill. If they came, Elsa could eat with them and make friends.

We pulled the buffalo into the shade of a tree and left Elsa there with it. In the morning we returned. Elsa was full with meat from the buffalo but there was no sign of other lions. We left her a second night with no more luck. By then the meat was very smelly. There seemed to be no lions around but there were many hyenas and vultures. They were waiting as near as they dared until Elsa would leave the dead animal.

We decided to leave the buffalo to the hyenas and get a fresh kill for Elsa. Quite near our camp George shot a buck. We left Elsa with it and returned to camp.

From inside our tent we heard Elsa pulling the heavy kill along the ground. I knew what she was trying to do; she wanted to bring her kill into the tent. But we kept her out. Poor Elsa, it was much safer inside the tent. Now she had to spend the whole night looking after her kill.

She did the best thing she could. She pulled the buck as near as she could. As a result the hyenas came so close and made so much noise that sleep was impossible.

In the end, Elsa got tired of keeping the hyenas away from her kill. We heard her pulling the buck towards the river and then splashing through the water with it. The hyenas stopped their noise and left. Did Elsa know they would not follow her through water?

She had no mother to teach her but she seemed to know so much. We took new hope from this adventure. Perhaps we could soon leave her to look after herself.

One afternoon Elsa refused to come for a walk with us. When we returned after dark she was gone. She did not return until early next morning. Later we found the marks of a large lion close to the tent.

When Elsa came back again I noticed that she had that certain strong smell about her. She was ready to mate again. Her condition showed in the way she acted towards us. She was friendly, but the real show of love was missing. Soon after breakfast she went off again and kept away all day.

After dark we heard her jumping on to the roof of the Landrover. I went out at once to play with her, but she was cool towards me and very restless. She jumped down and disappeared into the dark.

During the night I heard her splashing in the river. Loud sounds of anger and fear came from the baboons. This lasted until early morning, then Elsa returned for a quick visit to the camp. She let George hold her for a while. Then she growled in a friendly way and went off again.

It was clear that she was in love. We knew now that her condition would last about four days. This seemed to be the right time for us to leave her. We hoped that she would not be alone but with a mate. We decided to go away for one week and at once we began to get our things together.

While we were taking down the tent Elsa returned.

"You look after her," said George. "We'll get everything in the car. We'll go about a kilometre away and then I'll send Nuru to come and get you."

I took Elsa away from the camp to our tree beside the river. Was this the last time we would see it together? I tried to appear happy. But Elsa knew there was something wrong. I took the typewriter with me and sat under the tree on my usual seat. I hoped the noise of the typewriter would hide my unhappiness. I thought I was prepared for this moment. I knew Elsa would have a happier future in the wild. But it was very difficult to make the break now, and leave her. I think Elsa sensed my feelings and she rested her golden head against me.

The river moved slowly in front of us. A bird called; some dry leaves fell off the tree and were carried away by the water. Elsa was part of this life. She belonged to nature and not to man. We were 'man', we loved her, and we knew that she loved us. Would she be able to forget her life with us? Would she go and hunt when she was hungry? Or would she wait for our return knowing that we always took care of her?

It needed all the strength of my love for her to leave her now and give her back to nature. As I kissed her, Nuru came and called me. He had some meat for Elsa which she took and began to eat. We went quietly away.

# 7 We Leave Elsa

We drove twenty-five kilometres to another river, smaller but much deeper than the first. Here we planned to stay a week. Late in the afternoon George and I walked alongside the water. We walked quietly, our thoughts with Elsa. I felt deeply how close we all were. It was lonely with no Elsa walking by my side. I missed the feel of her soft skin and warm body. There was of course the hope of seeing her again in one week's time. How much that meant to me!

Suddenly George stopped, pointing ahead and we dropped to the ground. A hippo and her young one were feeding in the long grass beside the river. The sun was still too hot for them to leave the cool water. So the hippos kept comfortable with the water nearly over their backs, and ate the tasty leaves.

We watched this peaceful sight, but my heart was with Elsa. Then I noticed an elephant on the far side of the river. Only a few metres of water lay

between us. He was the leader of a small group which now came silently to the water's edge.

The river side was rocky. One by one each elephant drank its fill. Each one carefully stepped back to make way for the next thirsty animal. All this time the group stood close together round two very small elephants. Their great bodies kept away all possible danger.

The sun was going down, throwing its warm golden light on the tree-tops. Again I thought of Elsa – what a beautiful world she belonged to! We must do everything possible to give her back to all this beauty, I thought. We knew of no other lion returning successfully to its natural life after living with men. We were trying to do something quite new. We still hoped that Elsa would succeed.

At last the week of worry ended and we went back to see how Elsa was managing. When we arrived at our old camp we looked at once for her marks. There was no sign of them. I began to call. Soon afterwards we heard her friendly 'hnk-hnk' and saw her running to us from the river.

Her welcome showed us that she missed us as much as we missed her. We had a buck for her, but she only gave it a look and continued to cover us with love.

As soon as the great welcome was over I looked at her body. She was full.

"She must have eaten not long ago," I said to George. "I wonder what it was?"

All my worries left my mind. Elsa was now safe. Her fullness proved that she could get food without our help. While the tents were being put up I took her to the river and there we rested together. I was happy now, feeling that Elsa's future was a safe one. She seemed to feel the same. She rested her big soft head against me and went to sleep.

When she woke she still showed no interest in the buck. I then thought: "Where are our noisy friends, the baboons?" Later on I realised the truth about Elsa's first kill. We found bits of baboon hair close to their usual drinking place.

Now that our minds were at peace about Elsa's future we decided to spend a last few days with her. We hoped it would make our last goodbyes less difficult.

Elsa did not often let us out of her sight. When we were on our walks she only left us a few times to hunt for an hour by herself.

The country was becoming very dry and often the sky was lit up by grass fires. The short rains would come in the next two or three weeks. The dusty ground was thirsty for its life-giving water.

We took Elsa out of the camp for the whole day. We did not want her to live too closely with us as before. After an early morning walk of two or three hours we found a shady place along the river. We picnicked and I took out my drawing-book. Elsa soon went to sleep and I often rested against her when I read or slept.

George spent most of the time fishing and usually caught our lunch in the river. Elsa always tasted the first fish. After she tried a mouthful, she then pulled a face. After that she showed no more interest in the rest of George's catch. Nuru, who was a very good cook, cooked the fish quickly when it was caught.

One night we heard a lot of elephant noise. I was a bit worried when we started out on our usual walk early next morning. Elephants are the only big wild animals I am really afraid of. Elsa took the lead. She smelled the wind and chose to go in the direction of the elephants. Suddenly, her head came up and she went off at a fast run, leaving us behind. A few moments later, from far away, we heard the call of a lion.

Elsa stayed away all that day. Late in the evening we heard her call and another lion's call – both far away. During the night there were many hyenas about. They kept us awake with their loud empty laughter. At daybreak we went out and looked for Elsa's marks on the ground. We found them together with the marks of the other lion.

The next day we found her marks alone. On the fourth day we followed her across the river. We searched for her all that day until suddenly we were in the middle of a group of elephants. There was nothing to do but run!

Early on the fifth morning Elsa returned very hungry. She ate and ate until she could hold no more. After that she got on to my camp-bed and made it clear that we should leave her in peace. Later I noticed two deep bites on her back legs. I cleaned these as well as I could and Elsa seemed thankful.

In the afternoon she did not want to go for a walk. Instead she sat on the roof of the Landrover until dark, then she disappeared into the night. About two hours later we heard a lion and Elsa's answering call. At first the sound of her voice came from near the camp. But then we heard it again coming from the direction of the lion.

The following morning we decided that this was a good moment to leave Elsa alone for another few days. We moved camp, thinking that her wild lion friend might not like us near. We knew now that Elsa could look after herself and so this goodbye was less hurtful than the first one. But I was worried about her bites which looked a little unhealthy.

After a week we returned to our camping-place. We came upon Elsa as she was hunting two water buck. It was early in the afternoon and very hot. Poor thing, she must have been very hungry to be hunting so late in the day. She gave us a warm welcome and ate all the meat we had for her.

That night we heard a lion call and Elsa disappeared into the darkness and was away for two days. During this time she returned for one quick visit to George's tent. She was very loving and nearly broke his camp-bed by sitting on top of him as he lay asleep. After a short meal she went off again.

In the morning we followed her marks which led us to a rocky hill near the camp. We climbed to the top and looked unsuccessfully for her. In the end we nearly fell over her in some thick grass. Clearly she was keeping quiet in the hope that we would not see her. But she still showed her usual friendliness. We understood her feelings and left her alone.

Late that evening we heard the roar of a lion and the noise of the hyenas that followed him. Soon Elsa's voice sounded close to camp. Perhaps by now she knew to keep away from her mate while he was at his kill. Later she returned to George's tent for a few moments. She put her head on his leg and growled softly.

"You know I love you," she seemed to be saying. "But I have a friend to whom I *must* go. I hope you will understand." Then she was off again. Early next morning we found the marks of a big lion close to the camp. He must have waited there while Elsa went to George's tent to explain things.

She kept away for three days. Each evening she returned for a few minutes to say hello. Then she left again without touching the meat which was ready for her. Was she telling us that she wanted to leave us without hurting us?

During the night we were awakened by loud

lion growls and the laughing of hyenas. We listened, thinking Elsa would come in at any moment. But morning came and she did not return.

When it became light we went in the direction of the night's noises. After a few hundred metres we stopped suddenly. The growl of a lion came from the river below us. At the same time we saw a buck and some baboons racing away.

We moved carefully through the thick grass down to the river. In the sand there we found the fresh marks of at least two or three lions; they led across the river. We went across and followed the still wet marks on the other side. Not fifty metres away, through the trees, I noticed the shape of a lion.

While I looked hard to see if it was Elsa, George called to her. She walked away from us. When George repeated his call she only ran faster. Soon we saw only the black end of her tail through the trees.

We looked at each other. She must have heard us. Was she leaving us? Was she deciding her future at last and following the lions? Did this mean success?

We returned to camp alone, and very sad. Should we leave her now to live her own life? But George thought that we should wait a few more days to make sure that Elsa was accepted by the pride.

When she did not appear we decided to go back to Isiolo.

## 8 Elsa's New Life

Several weeks after our return to Isiolo, George arrived home one evening after a long tour of the lowland country where Elsa now lived with her mate. He brought exciting news.

"I've seen them," he told me. "Both of them. In fact, I saw them mating."

It was a month since the mating, when we set off in the Landrover. I was really afraid that Elsa would now follow her mate into a world beyond our reach.

She was waiting near our old camping-place when we arrived.

Instead of the excited welcome she usually gave us, she walked slowly up to me. She did not seem to be hungry and was unusually gentle and quiet. Feeling her head, I noticed that her skin was very soft and her coat very shiny. The reason was clear. She was going to have cubs. She must have become pregnant when she mated with her lion a month ago.

For two days she remained in camp with us. She ate such big meals that she was too sleepy to move till the afternoon when she went fishing with George. During the third night she ate so much that we were worried about her. That night she slept in front of my tent. Just before daybreak her lion started calling her and she went off in his direction.

George and I talked over plans to help her until her cubs were born.

"She won't be able to hunt in her condition," I said. "A pregnant lioness is usually helped by one or two other lionesses in the pride. I've heard that they act like 'aunts'. They are supposed to bring food and help with the new-born cubs. Her mate won't be any help at a time like this. In fact she probably won't let him near the cubs for some weeks."

"I don't think she's found a pride yet," George said. "I've only seen signs of the mate."

"If she has no 'aunts', we shall have to do their job. Let me stay here with Nuru for a while. We can get food for her if she needs it."

George agreed. He would visit us as often as his work let him.

Elsa seemed to have understood our conversation and jumped on to my camp-bed as soon as it was made ready. She seemed to think it was the only place for someone in her condition.

From now on she thought the bed was hers. The next morning Nuru carried it down beside the river for me because I didn't feel well. Elsa came to lie with me. This was uncomfortable, so after a time I pushed her off. Her feelings were hurt and she took herself off to the tall grass by the river.

It was late afternoon when I called her for a walk. Looking hard at me she walked straight up to my bed and stepped on to it. There she lifted her tail and did something which showed just how she felt about my action. Then with a very pleased look she jumped down and took the lead on our walk.

Now that she had taught me a lesson, it seemed, everything was all right between us.

As the days went by I noticed that her movements became very slow. Even the noise of elephants close by only made her lift her ears. She did not answer the call of her lion who seemed to be very near the camp.

Early one morning when the lion was calling we took Elsa for a walk in his direction. There, to our surprise, we found the marks of two lions. When Elsa began to show an interest in these marks we left her and returned home. She did not come back that night nor the following day. Was it possible she was making the friends that she so needed?

George shot a buck and left it as a parting present. He hoped that would make the lions

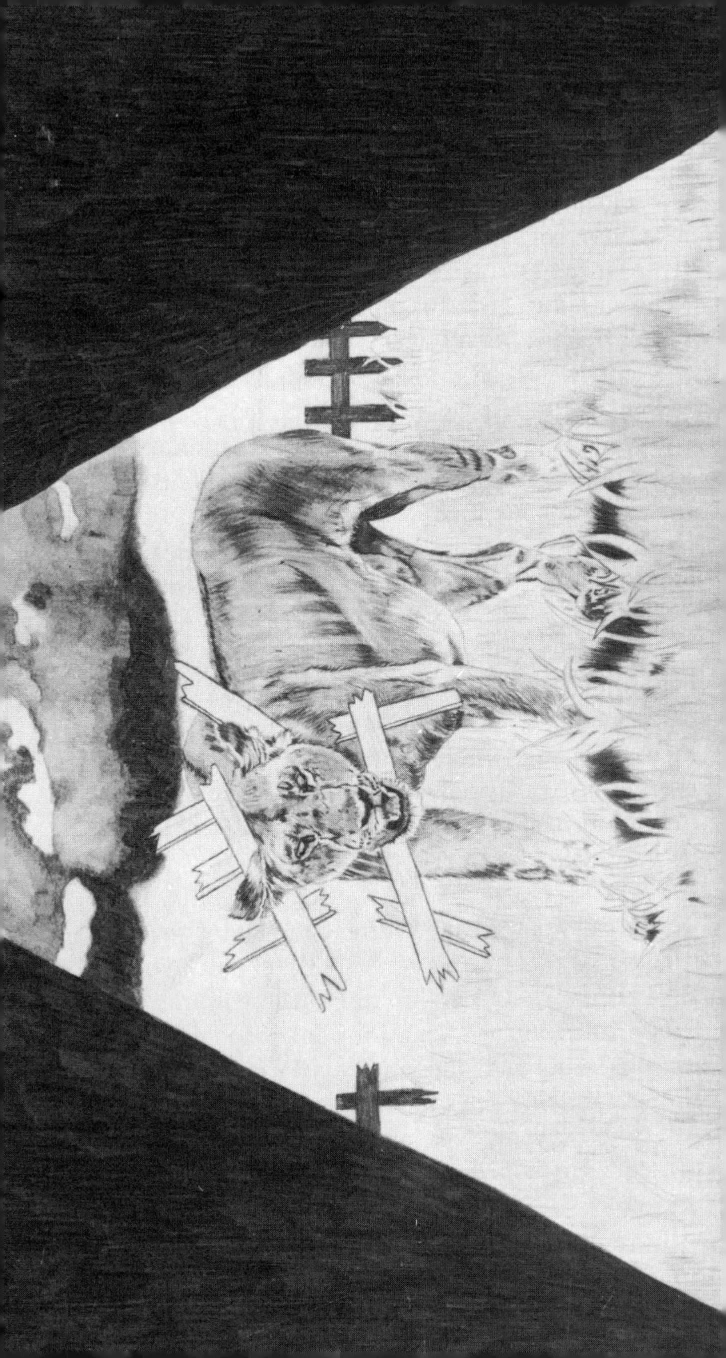

friendly towards her. Then we returned to Isiolo. We spent two weeks at home and then decided it was time to go and see Elsa again. It was dark when we reached camp, but Elsa appeared within a few moments. She was very thin, very hungry and had deep, bleeding bites on her neck and her back.

While she ate the meat we gave her I cleaned the bites. She thanked me by leaning her head against mine.

During the night we heard her pulling the buck meat down to the river and swimming across with it, and later we heard her returning. Very early in the morning she tried to push her way through the gate of the fence around my tent. She managed to push her head half-through but then got caught. The fight to free herself caused the gate to break off and she entered wearing it round her neck. I freed her at once but she seemed restless and in need of our comfort. We were still her 'pride'.

We spent a week in camp that time and then returned to Isiolo for two weeks. We continued like this until Elsa was nearly ready to give birth to her cubs.

Elsa was so heavy now that every movement seemed difficult. We wondered what place she would choose for the birth. We even thought that she might choose our tent. She always felt safe there.

I read all the books I could find on animal birth.

I was very afraid that something might go wrong.

We also had the fear that her lion would grow tired of waiting while she spent so much time with us. We didn't want him to leave. Elsa's cubs must have a father if they were to grow up wild.

Then one night Elsa came in the dark and spent the night close to my bed. This was something which she didn't often do now. I took it as a sign that she felt her time was near.

The next day when George and I went for a walk Elsa followed us. But she had to sit down often and was clearly in a lot of pain. When we saw this we turned back and walked very slowly. Suddenly, to our surprise, she turned away and left us.

There was nothing we could do to help her and we went back to camp.

For three days we waited. We saw and heard nothing of Elsa but we often heard her mate who stayed quite close to the camp. We left meat for him near the river. He pulled it away and we wondered if he was taking it to Elsa. We saw no sign of her near the river, the only place where she could get water, and this worried us greatly.

Another two days passed and we were silently eating our midday meal, each busy with our own thoughts. Suddenly there was a quick movement. Before I understood what was happening Elsa was between us, knocking everything off the table, pushing us to the ground, sitting on us and covering us with her loving tongue.

She was no longer pregnant and she looked in very good health. We gave her some meat which she ate at once.

Meanwhile we asked each other many questions. Why was she visiting us during the hottest part of the day, a time when she usually never moved? Did she choose this time to leave her cubs because no enemy would be about in such heat? Or were the cubs dead? And why did she wait for five days to come to us for food?

After a good meal and a long drink she walked towards the river and lay down for a sleep. We left her alone so that she would rest. When I looked for her at tea-time she was gone.

During the night we heard her lion calling from the other side of the river but we did not hear her answer.

We began to worry about the cubs. We felt we must know about them. The next morning we searched for five hours but we found nothing.

We carried on equally unsuccessfully in the afternoon. Then we heard Nuru firing a gun, a signal that Elsa was in camp.

She was very loving when we got back. She ate a great meal and lay down, showing no sign of returning to her cubs. This worried me because it was getting dark and this was the worst time to leave them alone.

Later she went back to her meal and carefully cleaned up every bit of it. Then at last she disappeared into the dark. Very likely she waited till there was no light to make sure we could not follow her.

Realising this, we felt sure that she was looking after her cubs. But we could not be happy until we saw for ourselves that they were healthy and safe.

We had to wait several days before Elsa let that happen.

On one of our searches we called loudly for her for about half an hour. She suddenly appeared out of some rocks only twenty metres away. She did not seem pleased at our nearness and looked at us silently without moving. After a few moments she sat down with her back to us. She was clearly saying, "Here my own world begins and you must not enter it."

We left her some meat and went away as she wished.

Even now we searched every day. Several times we thought we must be very near the cubs. Each time Elsa appeared. Sometimes she came to say hello and pushed me to the ground. It was a friendly push but it meant, "Don't come any closer."

Another time she came to us out of the grass and silently led us back to camp. As she walked she looked over her shoulder to make sure we were following her. She ate the meat we gave her at the camp but would not let me touch her. She made me feel like a spy and I felt I must stop my searching.

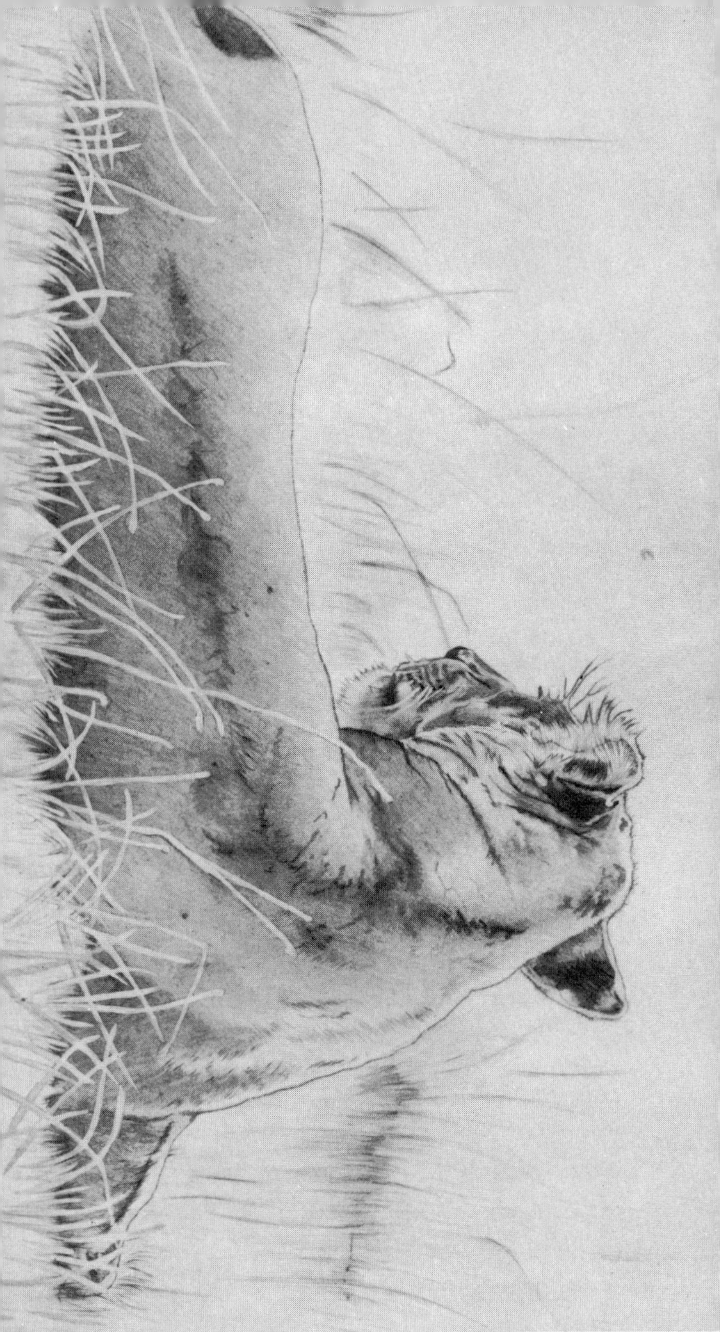

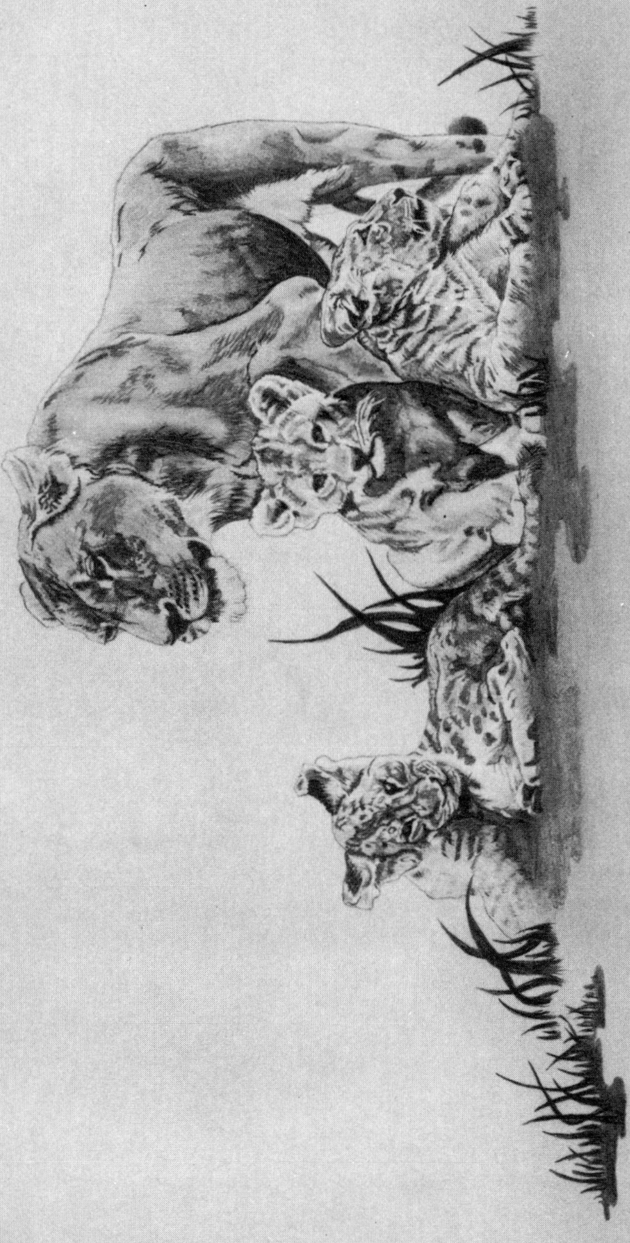

Still, she needed the food that we brought her. I did not know what to do for the best. If I continued to leave food close to her hiding-place, would it not bring enemies? On the other hand if I kept the meat in camp Elsa had to leave her cubs to come and get it. The cubs might be killed while she was absent.

One evening while I was writing near the river my worries came to an end. Elsa was calling in a very strange voice from the other side of the river. I ran to the river bank and there stopped unable to believe my eyes.

There was Elsa standing on a sandbank within a few metres of me. One cub stood close to her, a second cub was climbing out of the water shaking itself dry and a third stood calling to his mother from the far bank.

I remained very still while Elsa returned to the far bank and brought the third cub across in her mouth. I did not move as she walked slowly to me and gently pushed her head into my hand. She wanted to show her cubs that we were friends.

The cubs watched with interest but decided to stay just out of my reach. I wanted to bend forward and touch them but I stopped myself. Never touch cubs until they want you to.

I sat down carefully and Elsa lay down beside me. The cubs ran to her. They pressed their fat little bodies against her and began to drink their mother's milk.

We all sat together on the grass and there was not a sound except for the cubs feeding. I did not know what the future would bring but I would never forget the happiness that Elsa gave me that evening.

# A Crossword

We hope you enjoy this crossword. All the answers come from the story.
There's a hidden word that goes from one corner to another. It's the name of something that lives in Kenya. Can you find it?

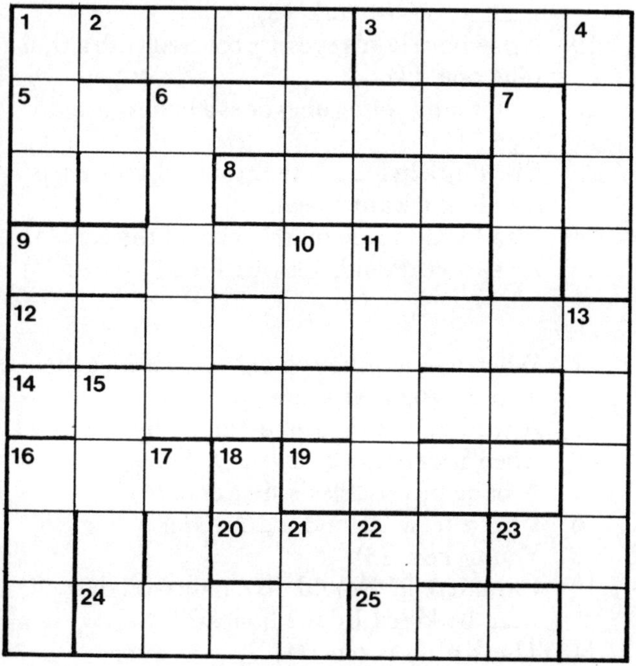


*Across*

1 In a mating condition, Elsa's body had a strange one. (5)
3 The man-eater's teats were heavy with it. (4)

5 My husband looks after wild life, and has to hunt dangerous animals. (2)
6 Group of lions. (5)
8 Our boy. (4)
9 It was about 200km southwest of Isiolo. (7)
12 Our car. (9)
14 An impala is one. (8)
16 Elsa sometimes washed my face before she ____ me start work. (3)
19 A newborn lion's eyes are covered with a thin blue one. (4)
20 How many young ones does a lioness usually have? (4)
23 Elsa dug a hole ____ the ground for the parts she didn't want to eat. (2)
24 Elsa liked to ride on this part of the car. (4)
25 At two years old, Elsa was ready for it. (3)

*Down*

1 When a lioness has young, ____ brings their food for the first year. (3)
2 A wild animal is usually killed by others when it carries the smell of these. (3)
4 A baboon was Elsa's first one. (4)
6 I liked to write and ____ under a tree. (5)
7 Young lion. (3)
10 I wondered, "Would Elsa mate with the lion, ____ be killed by the lioness?" (2)
11 The Koran is one. (4)
13 A dangerous animal that we met. (5)
15 I often watched wild animals from a tree ____ the river. (4)
16 Nature's is hard. (3)

17 How many cubs do you usually see with a lioness? (3)

18 Elsa would be dead ____ the cubs had stayed in the wild. (2)

21 Elsa started to eat a kill at the inside part ____ the back legs. (2)

22 When Elsa left with the elephants, I was worried until she came safely back to ____. (2)

## Answers

*Across*

1 smell 3 milk 5 he 6 pride 8 Nuru 9 Nairobi 12 Landrover 14 antelope 16 let 19 skin 20 four 23 in 24 roof 25 sex

*Down*

1 she 2 men 4 kill 6 paint 7 cub 10 or 11 book 13 rhino 15 near 16 law 17 two 18 if 21 of 22 us